AF599112

ON THE HUNT

PHEASANT HUNTING

BY ROXANNE TROUP

EPIC

BELLWETHER MEDIA • MINNEAPOLIS, MN

This edition first published in 2025 by Bellwether Media, Inc.

Library of Congress Cataloging-in-Publication Data

LC record for Pheasant Hunting available at: https://lccn.loc.gov/2024037670

Editor: Elizabeth Neuenfeldt Designer: Jeffrey Kollock

Printed in the United States of America, North Mankato, MN.

TABLE OF CONTENTS

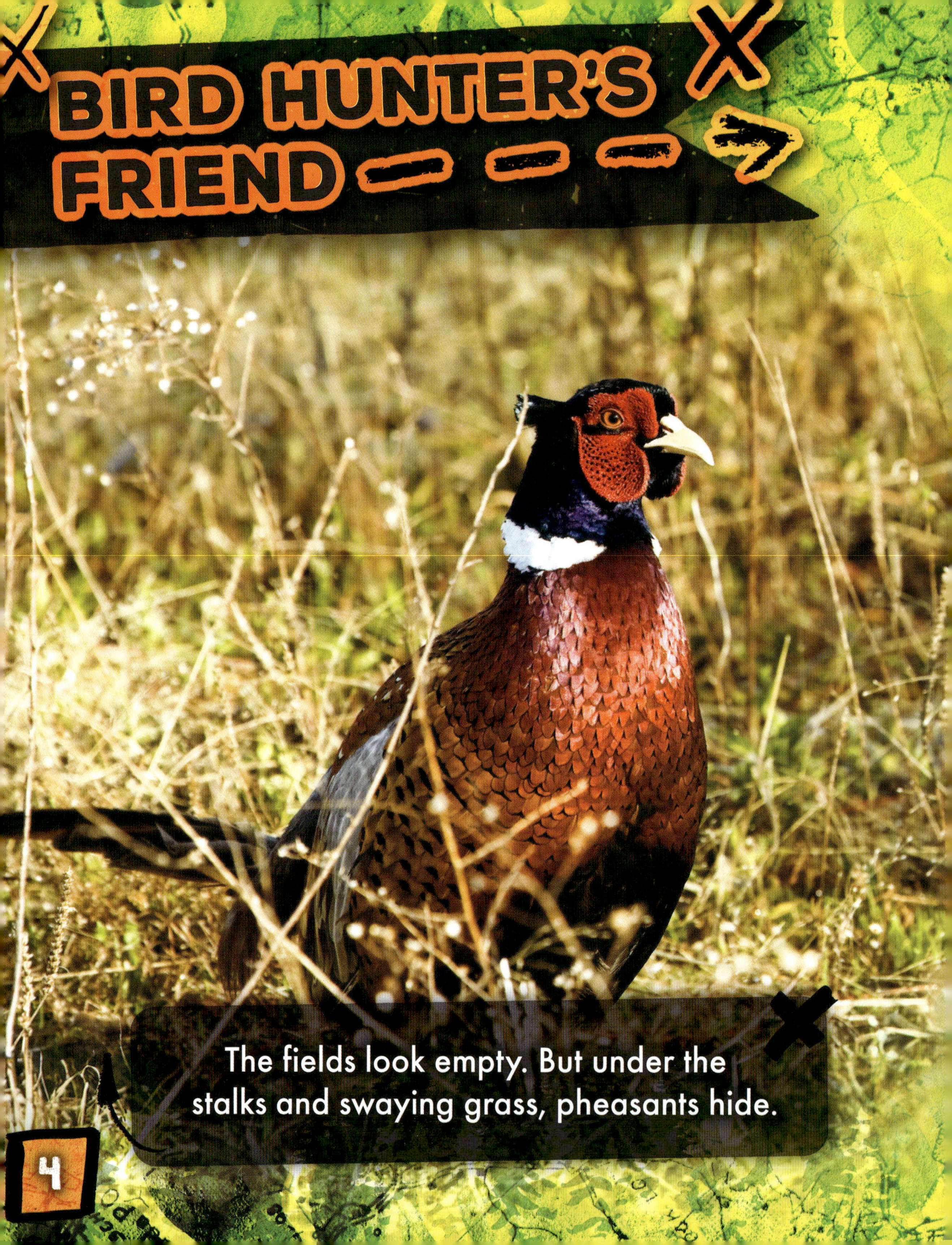

BIRD HUNTER'S FRIEND

The fields look empty. But under the stalks and swaying grass, pheasants hide.

A **bird dog** catches their scent. It **points**. Then it waits. On command, it rushes the grass. A pheasant flies. The hunter takes aim. Boom!

WHAT IS PHEASANT HUNTING?

Pheasants are birds that live in **prairies** and **marshes**. They are hunted in the fall and winter.

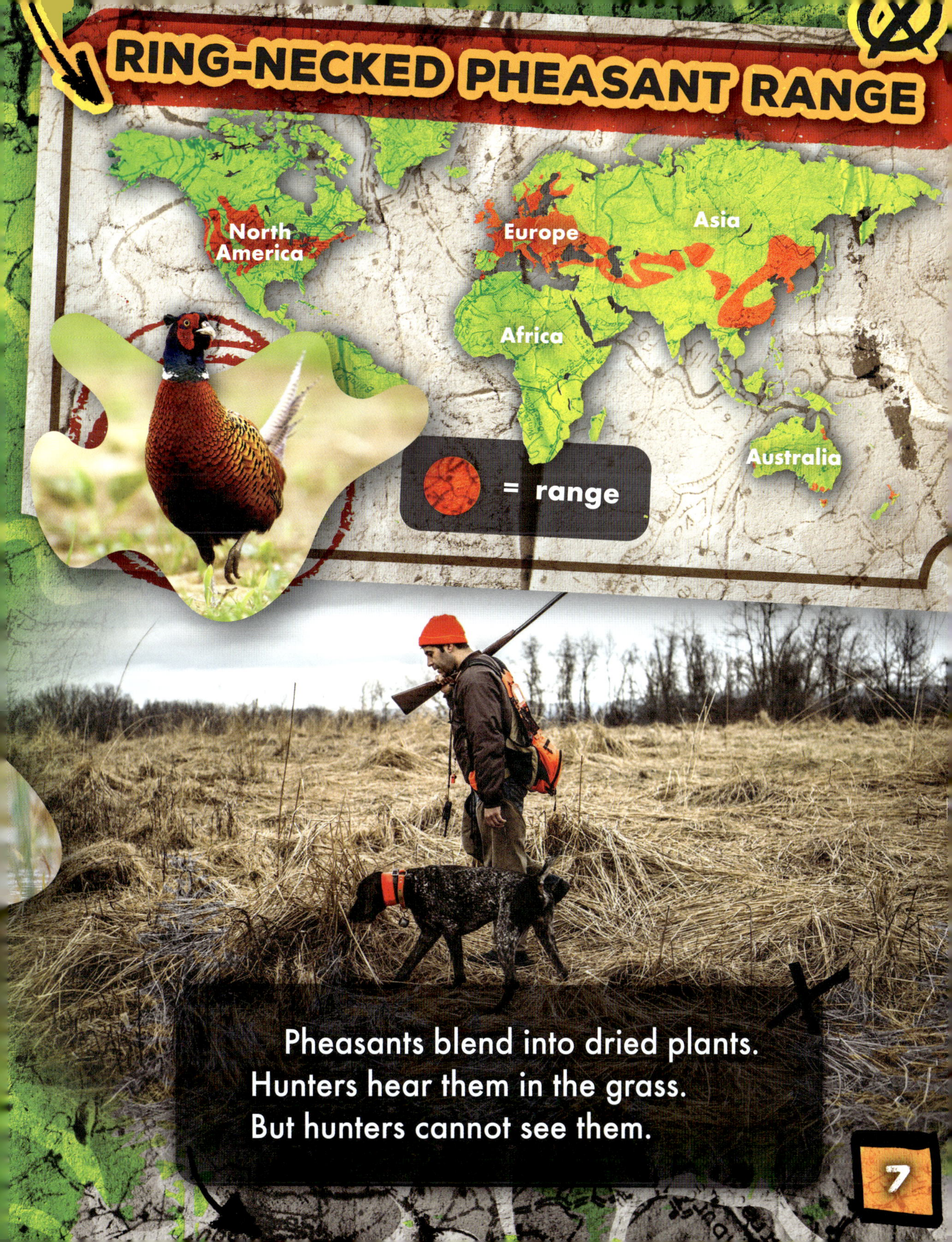

Pheasants blend into dried plants.
Hunters hear them in the grass.
But hunters cannot see them.

Many pheasant hunters use dogs to help them hunt. Bird dogs are trained to sniff out and **retrieve** hunted birds.

Other hunters work with friends. They search fields in a zig-zag pattern to **flush** the birds.

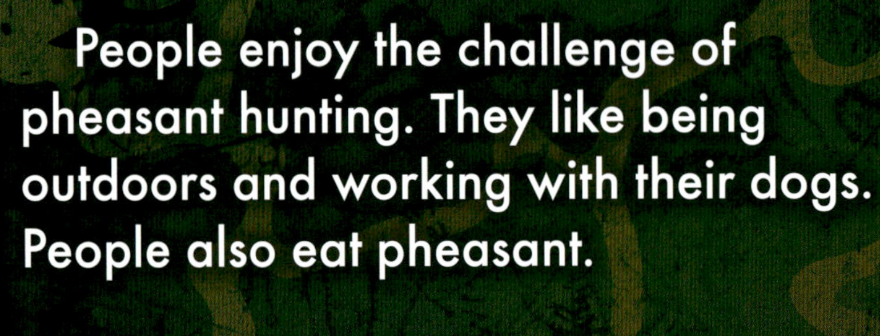

People enjoy the challenge of pheasant hunting. They like being outdoors and working with their dogs. People also eat pheasant.

The **Great Plains** are a popular place to hunt. They have public land and **walk-in ground** for hunting.

FAVORITE HUNTING SPOT

LAKE OAHE

Over **2,250** miles (3,621 kilometers) of shoreline open to hunting

Great Plains

PREPARING TO HUNT

Hunters need a shotgun and plenty of **nontoxic ammo**.

Pheasants only fly short distances. But they are fast. Hunters often miss their shots.

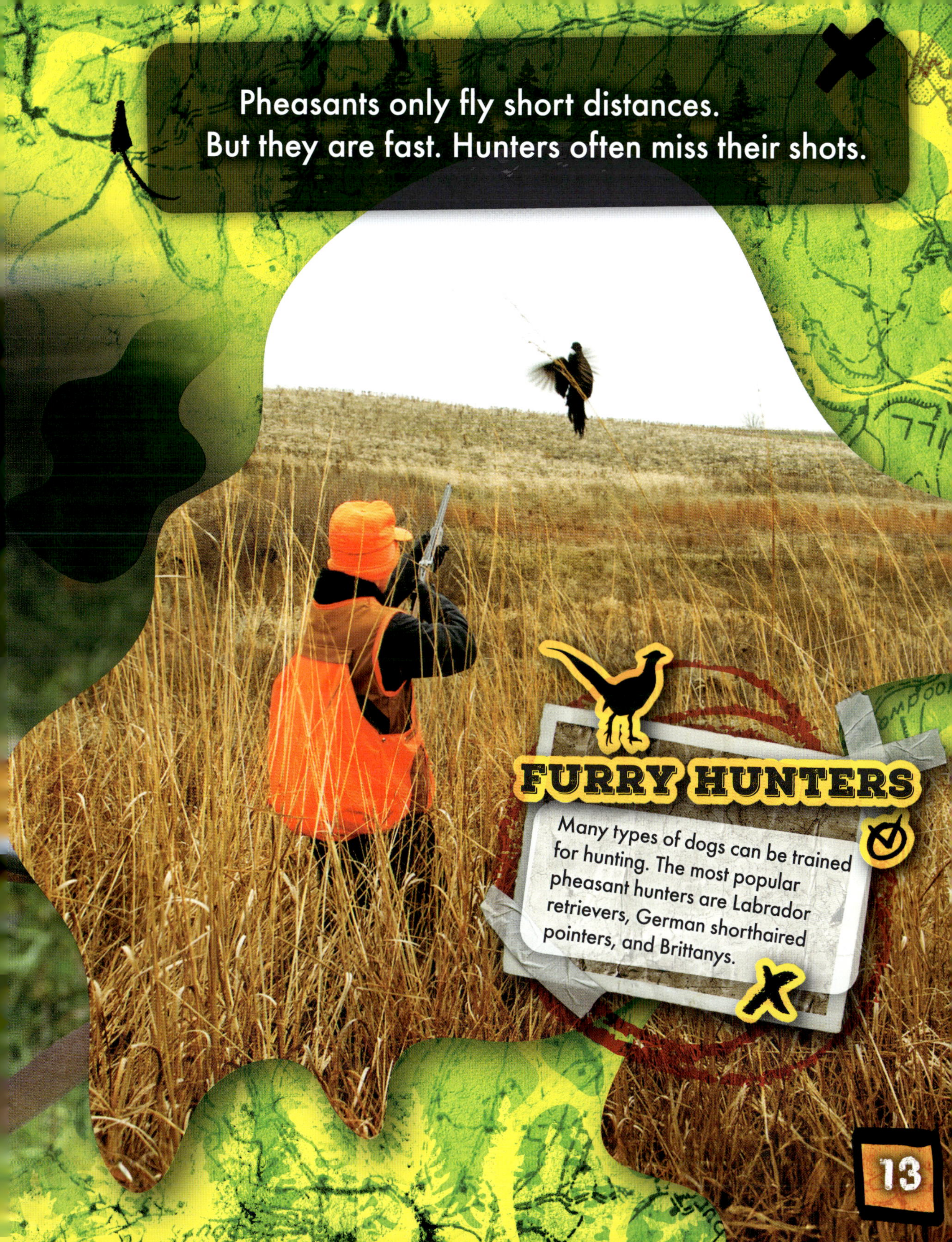

FURRY HUNTERS

Many types of dogs can be trained for hunting. The most popular pheasant hunters are Labrador retrievers, German shorthaired pointers, and Brittanys.

Hunters wear sturdy shoes and pants. This protects them from weeds and brush. They wear **blaze orange** so other hunters can see them.

Most hunters wear **upland vests**. These vests help hunters carry downed birds and supplies.

Many hunters like to wear shooting glasses. These protect their eyes from brush and dirt.

HUNTING GEAR

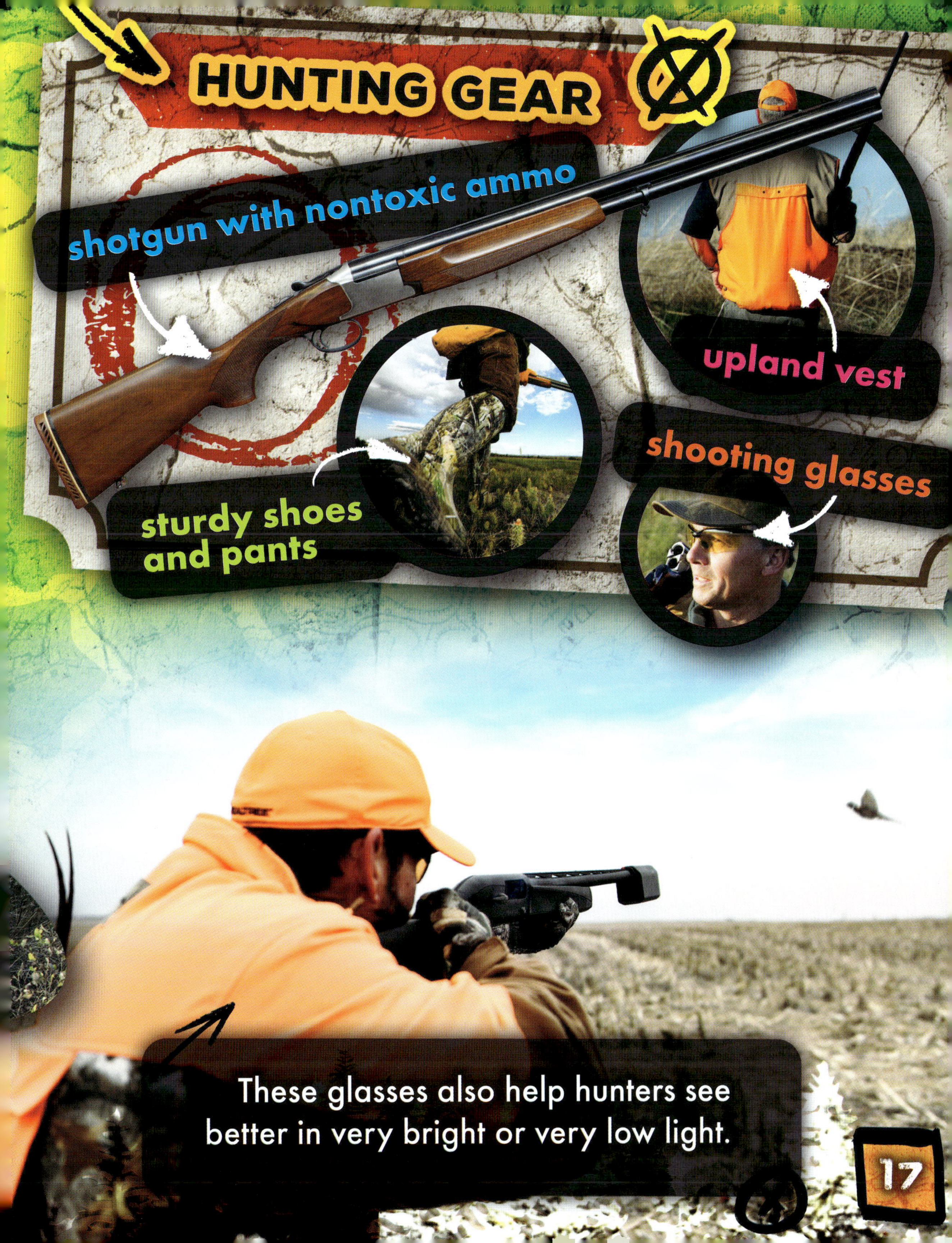

These glasses also help hunters see better in very bright or very low light.

RULES OF THE HUNT

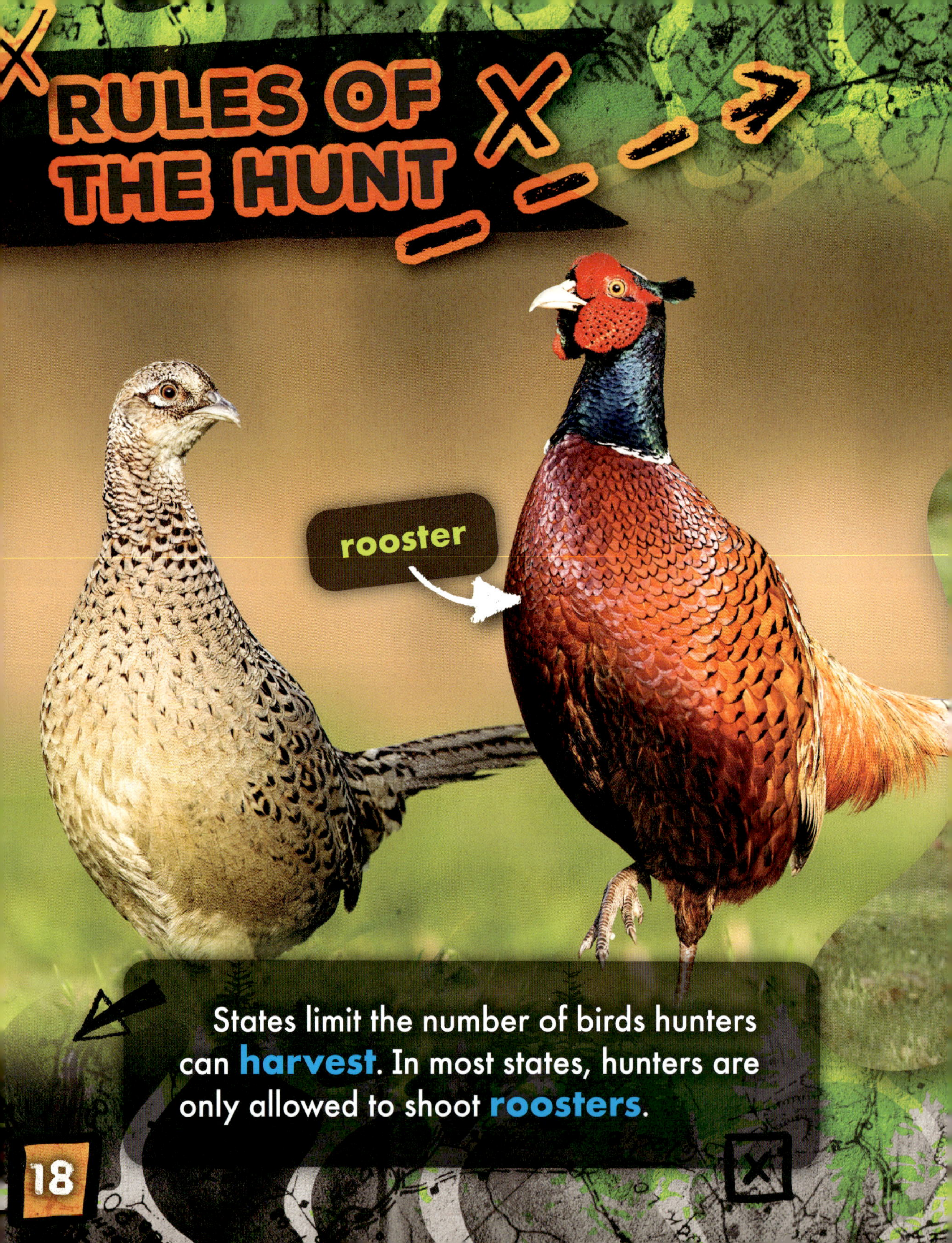

States limit the number of birds hunters can **harvest**. In most states, hunters are only allowed to shoot **roosters**.

People can only hunt within a set season. This keeps pheasant numbers high.

People need a **license** to hunt pheasants. They must handle a gun safely. They must make clean shots.

If hunters use bird dogs, the dogs should be well trained. This protects everyone!

gun safety class

GLOSSARY

bird dog—a dog trained to help hunters track, flush, and retrieve birds

blaze orange—a bright orange color that hunters wear for safety

flush—to scare a bird out of hiding

Great Plains—a region of flat or gently rolling land in the central United States

harvest—to collect

license—a document that gives hunters legal permission to harvest a certain type of animal

marshes—areas of wet land that have many types of plants

nontoxic ammo—ammo made with material that is not poisonous to animals

points—when a trained dog stops and points its nose toward a specific smell; pointing alerts its owner that a bird is nearby.

prairies—large grasslands that are mostly flat and treeless

retrieve—to bring something back

roosters—male pheasants

upland vests—vests worn by pheasant hunters to carry downed pheasants

walk-in ground—privately-owned land open to public hunting

TO LEARN MORE

AT THE LIBRARY

Bailey, Diane. *Bird Hunting*. Minneapolis, Minn.: Lerner Publications, 2024.

Coulson, Art. *Pheasant Hunting Firsts*. North Mankato, Minn.: Capstone Publishing, 2022.

Troup, Roxanne. *Duck Hunting*. Minneapolis, Minn.: Bellwether Media, 2025.

ON THE WEB

FACTSURFER

Factsurfer.com gives you a safe, fun way to find more information.

1. Go to www.factsurfer.com.
2. Enter "pheasant hunting" into the search box and click 🔍.
3. Select your book cover to see a list of related content.

INDEX

The images in this book are reproduced through the courtesy of: Marcin Perkowski, cover; photomaster, p. 3; Linda Hughes Photography, p. 4; Mountains Hunter, pp. 5, 12; Bridges Photography, p. 5 (pointing); WildMedia, pp. 6, 7 (range), 18; Tracy Immordino (prairie), p. 6; Jose Almeida Photography, p. 7; Vallorie Francis/ Alamy, pp. 8, 13; Acorns Resort/ Wikimedia Commons, p. 9; Traveller70, p. 10; Design Pics Inc/ Alamy, p. 11; Steve Bower, p. 11 (Great Plains); www.pqpictures.co.uk/ Alamy, p. 12 (ammo); JOHN HENNIGAN, pp. 14, 17 (upland vest); Nikolai Hamel/ Alamy, p. 15; MintImages, pp. 16, 17 (glasses); amurray175, p. 17; BearFotos, p. 17 (shotgun); OUTDOOR_MEDIA, p. 17 (shoes); Steve Oehlenschlager, p. 19; Wichita Eagle/ Getty Images, p. 20; ASSOCIATED PRESS/ AP Images, p. 21; Eric Isselee, p. 23.